The Christmas Adventure

An Improv Play about Jesus's Birth
for Children Ages 4-10

Jessica Bodiford

ACKNOWLEDGMENTS

I would like to send a big THANK YOU to Ayeke Messam, Leslie Carr-Robinson, Henri Ward, Alan Yarborough, and Nadly Belizaire for supporting me through my first published play with their comments and editing assistance.

I would like to thank the Shaw Temple AME Zion Church family for giving me the opportunity to create plays and make wonderful memories.

I would also like to express my gratitude to Josephine Marcellin-Maitre, Joanne Hill, and Shiltone Béon for believing in me and supporting me through the ups and downs of being a self-employed artist.

Lastly, I would like to thank all those who have been with me since I moved to Haiti. I could not have made it this far without you.

God's blessings are abundant!

.

Tips for the Director

Before the first rehearsal, the actors playing the Adventurers should learn their lines. Give the actors the script a few days before the first rehearsal so they can memorize their lines. Knowing the lines beforehand will greatly reduce the number of rehearsals.

Record the Adventures' lines to help with memorization. Record the actors, who are playing the Adventurers, reading their lines. You can do simple recordings on a computer, cell phone, or tablet. After, give the actors the recordings to help them with memorization. Each actor can repeat their lines while playing the recording. This can also be done prior to the first rehearsal.

Props are necessary, but scenery is optional. The props are easy to find (or make). They are fun for the children. Feel free to use scenic elements, but the props are enough to keep the child's imagination flowing.

The props include:
- A big bag for the Adventurers to store most of the other props (except for the doll and the manger)
- Manger with a baby Jesus doll hidden inside
- Angel wings
- Pregnant costume piece for Mary

- Stuffed animals for shepherds
- Star
- Tambourines
- Scholarly caps
- Rock
- Shoe
- NIV Bible

Sound effects add to the story. Sound effects add to the play's ambience. In past productions, I have used the following:

- High energy music to start the show.
- A sound every time Adventurer 2 interrupts Adventurer 1 and says "Wait!"
- A few bars of the *Wedding March* for Mary and Joseph when Adventurer 2 says, "Now, Mary and Joseph can get married."
- Galloping sounds when the actors and audience are on the donkeys.
- Animal sounds for each animal in the stable.
- A chime sound for every time Adventurer 2 says, "Look, the star!"
- Music to end the show.

Sound effects can be done with voices, instruments, and/or recordings.

Create memorized roles for children. If there are children interested in having memorized parts for *The Christmas Adventure*, consider:

- Including children in the show's opening and closing. For example, the children's choir can sing a song at the beginning of the show, a group can introduce the show, the 4 and 5-year-olds can lead the church in a memorized prayer, or a group of children can present the actors during the curtain call.
- Choreographing an angel dance for children to perform when Adventurer 1 says, "Glory to God in the highest."
- Having the children do sound effects for the play.
- Having the children recite the Bible verses in the play (John 3:16, Mark 10:14). The Adventures would invite them to speak instead of reading the verses with children chosen from the audience.

The options are limitless. Remember, memorized roles for children are not required for this play, but there must be children in the audience to play the improvisational roles.

Have a practice run in front of a few children, ages 4 -10. Rehearse using props and costumes for a few children who are unfamiliar with the play. This will give you a chance to watch the children's enthusiasm and help the Adventurers understand what adjustments they need to make.

Anywhere is a stage. This compact play can be performed at churches, schools, women & children shelters, the park, basically anywhere there are young children.

Seat the children as close to the stage as possible.
Seating the children close to the stage will shorten the
lag time between the actors inviting a child to play a
role and the child arriving onstage. If possible, have
the children sit on the stage itself.

Have a runner. The runner selects which children
come on stage. A runner is especially useful for
productions with large audiences. The runner can
also assist children going up and down stairs.

**Use microphones, especially for children invited to
speak.** Microphones magnify soft, hesitant, or unclear
voices. The microphones can also help the
Adventurers when performing for large crowds. If
you decide to use mics, remember to have the
Adventurers rehearse with them. The Adventurers
should practice speaking into microphones and
holding mics for the children invited on stage.

Characters:
ADVENTURER 1
ADVENTURER 2

Characters played by children in the audience:
MARY
ANGEL
JOSEPH
3 SHEPHERDS
STAR
2 TAMBOURINE SHAKERS
3 MAGI

The ADVENTURERS energetically run onto the stage. One of them is carrying a big bag of props.

ADVENTURER 1
It is great to see all the children! We need you to help us on this Christmas adventure. Can anybody tell me what Christmas is all about?

(A child is chosen to speak. No matter what the child says, the ADVENTURERS affirm the child's answer.)

ADVENTURER 2
Thank you for sharing with us!

ADVENTURER 1
Let me tell you. Christmas is when we celebrate baby

Jesus's birth. But this little baby ends up being the Savior of the entire world. Let us begin in a small town called Galilee. There was a young woman named Mary. God was very pleased with her, so he....

ADVENTURER 2
Wait!

ADVENTURER 1
Yes?

ADVENTURER 2
We need someone to play Mary!

ADVENTURER 1
Oopps, I totally forgot.
(To the children in the audience)
Is there anybody who thinks they can play Mary, Jesus's mom?

(A girl is chosen to play MARY)

ADVENTURER 2
(To ADVENTURER 1)
Now you may continue.

ADVENTURER 1
Thank you. Where was I...? Oh yes, there was a

young woman named Mary. God was very pleased with her, so he decided to do something miraculous through her. God sent an angel to....

ADVENTURER 2
Wait!

ADVENTURER 1
(A little annoyed)
Yes?

ADVENTURER 2
We need someone to play the angel.

ADVENTURER 1
I was getting to that.
(To the children in the audience)
Is there anybody who thinks they can play the angel?

(A child is chosen to play the ANGEL)

ADVENTURER 2
(Rummaging through the bag)
Let's see what I have in here. Here it is!
(Pulls out wings and puts them on the child playing the ANGEL)
These wings look very good on you.
(To ADVENTURER 1)
Now, you may continue.

ADVENTURER 1

God sent an angel to Mary. And the angel said....

ADVENTURER 2

(To the child playing the ANGEL)

Now you say this to Mary, "Greetings, you who are highly favored!"[1]

(The child playing the ANGEL will repeat the line)

ADVENTURER 1

But Mary was scared. Mary, you need to look scared!

(The ADVENTURERS encourage MARY to look scared)

ADVENTURER 2

(To the ANGEL)

But then you, the angel, say, "Don't be afraid, Mary, you have found favor with God."[2]

(The ANGEL repeats the line)

ADVENTURER 1

Then the angel continues telling Mary that she will give birth to a son named Jesus.

---

[1] Luke 1:28 NIV
[2] Luke 1:30 NIV

ADVENTURER 2

This was really weird because Mary was just a little country girl from Galilee. She wanted to know how this was going to happen. Mary, ask the angel, "How can this be?"

(MARY asks the ANGEL)

ADVENTURER 1

The angel explained how the Holy Spirit was going to overshadow Mary. Angel, remind Mary that nothing is impossible with God!

(The ANGEL reminds MARY that nothing is impossible with God)

ADVENTURER 1 (cont'd)

Mary believed what the angel said, and fell on her knees.
(Encourages MARY to fall on her knees)
And she says, "I am the Lord's servant."[3]
(Encourages MARY to say the line)
And the angel went away.
(To the ANGEL, pointing to a corner of the stage)
You can go over there. Bye bye for now, angel.

---

[3] Luke 1:38 NIV

ADVENTURER 2
Wait!

ADVENTURER 1
(Annoyed)
Yes!

ADVENTURER 2
What about Joseph, Mary's fiancé? I don't think he's going to be happy about this.

ADVENTURER 1
Let's see what happens.
(To the children in the audience)
Can we have somebody play Joseph?

(A boy is chosen. In the meantime, a costume piece is pulled from the bag. MARY wears the costume piece. It has something on the inside to make MARY look pregnant)

ADVENTURER 2
Joseph didn't like what he saw at all. He was just shaking his head because he didn't want to embarrass Mary.
(Shakes head to encourage JOSEPH to shake his head)
But he didn't know how she became pregnant.

ADVENTURER 1

But the angel of the Lord appeared to Joseph.
(To the child playing the ANGEL)
Come back angel. You say to Joseph, "Mary will give birth to a son who will save people from their sins."[4]

(The ANGEL repeats the line)

ADVENTURER 2

(To the children in the audience)
Does anybody know who the baby is that will save people from their sins? If you do, shout it out!

(The children in the audience should say, "Jesus!")

ADVENTURER 1

I can't hear you. Say, "Jesus," LOUDER!

(Children shout)

ADVENTURER 2

Thank you, angel, for sharing the good news. Now, Mary and Joseph can get married.
(To the ANGEL)
You can go back to your seat.

(Wings are retrieved from the child)

---

[4] Matthew 1:21 NIV

ADVENTURER 1
Let us continue. Joseph had to go to Bethlehem to be counted in the census.
(To the children in the audience)
Now everybody needs to stand up because we're going to take a long trip to Bethlehem with the newlywed couple.

ADVENTURER 2
Mary sat on a donkey because she was pregnant. Mary, you need to climb on the donkey, kind of like getting on a horse.

BOTH ADVENTURERS
Let's pretend!

ADVENTURER 1
(To the children in the audience)
We all need to get on our donkeys for this trip, too.

BOTH ADVENTURERS
Everybody climb on your donkeys!

ADVENTURER 2
Off to Bethlehem we go!

(ADVENTURERS climb on donkeys. Children will follow. ADVENTURERS do a "giddy up" motion)

BOTH ADVENTURERS
Giddy up, giddy up, giddy up, giddy up....

ADVENTURER 1
(Pulls the reins on donkey)
Whoa! I see an inn over there. Let's see if they have space for Mary and Joseph.

ADVENTURER 2
We all need to climb off our donkeys.

(ADVENTURERS climb off donkeys. Children will follow)

ADVENTURER 1
(Pointing towards the audience)
There's the innkeeper. Joseph, ask him if there is any room for you and your pregnant wife.

(JOSEPH asks the question. ADVENTURER 1 represents the innkeeper)

ADVENTURER 1 (cont'd)
(Wagging her finger and shaking her head)
The innkeeper said, "No, no, no." Sorry, Mary and Joseph, there is no space at this inn. We all need to get back on our donkeys to look for another inn. Everybody climb on your donkeys.

BOTH ADVENTURERS

Here we go!

(ADVENTURERS climb on donkeys. Children will follow. ADVENTURERS do a "giddy up" motion)

Giddy up, giddy up, giddy up, giddy up....

ADVENTURER 2

Oh no! Mary's donkey is tired. Pregnant women can be very heavy.

ADVENTURER 1

Maybe our donkeys can go for a little bit more.

BOTH ADVENTURERS

(At a slower pace)

Giddy up, giddy up, giddy up, giddy up....

ADVENTURER 1

(Pulls the reins on donkey)

Whoa! I see another inn.

ADVENTURER 2

Joseph, ask the innkeeper if there is any room for you and your pregnant wife.

(JOSEPH asks the innkeeper)

ADVENTURER 1

Finally, this innkeeper says there is room! Hurray!

Now everyone can sit down.

ADVENTURER 2
(To MARY and JOSEPH)
Sorry guys, you have to spend the night in the stable
with the animals.
(Pointing to the manger that is already onstage)
But it's okay, Jesus won't mind. What kind of animals
did they have in the stable?

ADVENTURER 1
There were chickens.
(To the children in the audience)
If you are 4, 5, or 6 years old cluck like chickens.

(The ADVENTURERS encourage the 4, 5, and 6-year-
olds to cluck like chickens)

ADVENTURER 2
Were there pigs in the stable?

ADVENTURER 1
Yes! If you are 7, 8, or 9 years old oink like a pig.

(The ADVENTURERS encourage the 7, 8, and 9-year-
olds to oink like pigs)

ADVENTURER 2
And cows? Were there cows in the stable?

ADVENTURER 1
If you are 10 or older, moo like a cow.

(The ADVENTURERS encourage the older kids to moo like cows)

ADVENTURER 2
Wow, there were a lot of animals in that stable. Can we hear all those animal sounds again?

(The ADVENTURERS encourage everyone to make the animal sounds)

ADVENTURER 2 (cont'd)
Thank you for all those animals!

ADVENTURER 1
After some time, Jesus was born. Look inside the manger, Mary, and show everybody Jesus.

(MARY takes a doll out of the manger and shows it to everyone)

ADVENTURER 1 (cont'd)
There were also some shepherds in this story. I need three shepherds.

(Three SHEPHERDS are chosen, and each one is handed a stuffed animal)

ADVENTURER 1 (cont'd)
The shepherds were watching their flocks by night. Then suddenly the angel of the Lord appeared! The shepherds were scared. Show us how scared you are shepherds.

(The SHEPHERDS act scared)

ADVENTURER 2
And the angel said,
(Acting as the angel)
"Do not be afraid. I have good news of great joy for all people. Today Christ the Savior is born."[5]

ADVENTURER 1
(To the children in the audience)
Everyone stand up because after the angel spoke, the entire sky was filled with a heavenly host. It was like a great big concert for the shepherds. We are all going to tell the shepherds,
(Waving her hands in big motions)
"Glory to God in the highest!"[6] Come on heavenly host, let's tell the shepherds.

---

[5] Luke 2:10-11 NIV
[6] Luke 2:14 NIV

("Glory to God in the highest!" is repeated three or four times with hand motions. Children in the audience will follow)

ADVENTURER 2
(Directing the SHEPHERDS to the manger)
Then the shepherds were so happy and went to find baby Jesus.
(To the SHEPHERDS)
Show us how happy you are! The shepherds couldn't wait to get back home to share the good news.
(To the children in the audience and to the SHEPHERDS)
And you can sit down.

(The SHEPHERDS return to their seats and the stuff animals are left at the manger)

ADVENTURER 1
There was also this really bright star over the stable where the precious baby Jesus lay. This star was special because it let people know that Jesus was born. We need someone to hold the star.

(A child is chosen and a big star is pulled from the bag)

ADVENTURER 1 (cont'd)
We also need two other people.

(Two children are chosen, and three tambourines are pulled from the bag. One tambourine is for each child and one is for ADVENTURER 2)

ADVENTURER 2
Now every time someone says, "Look, the star!" Shake your tambourines. You got it? Okay, let's try it. "Look, the star!"
(The kids and ADVENTURER 2 shake the tambourines)
Magnificent! You guys make excellent stars.

ADVENTURER 1
And there were three Magi. They were really smart people who followed the star to find Jesus. Who can play a Magi?

(Three children are chosen to play MAGI. Scholarly caps are pulled out of the bag. The MAGI wear them on their heads)

ADVENTURER 2
It took a while for the Magi to find Jesus. I think the Magi need some help.
(To the children in the audience)
Look from left to right to help the Magi search for the star. And the Magi searched, and they searched, and they searched, and finally…
(Pointing at one of the MAGI)

…one of them said, "Look, the star!"

(The MAGI says the line. ADVENTURER 2 shakes tambourine. The children with the tambourines might make noise)

ADVENTURER 1
Where's the star? I don't see anything. I don't hear anything.

ADVENTURER 2
Say, "Look, the star," louder! And show my friend the star.

(Children do this. Tambourines are ringing)

ADVENTURER 1
Oh, I see it!

BOTH ADVENTURERS
We know where baby Jesus is!

ADVENTURER 2
(To the children with the tambourines and star)
Thank you for helping me show the Magi where baby Jesus is. Now you may take a seat.

(Tambourines and star are retrieved from the children)

ADVENTURER 1
Let's go to see Jesus….

ADVENTURER 2
Wait!

ADVENTURER 1
(Annoyed)
We're almost done!

ADVENTURER 2
The Magi need to bring gifts to Jesus.

ADVENTURER 1
Oh yes, I almost forgot. It took a while for the Magi to figure out good gifts. I think the Magi need some help.
(Tapping her finger on her chin and tapping her foot)
Do like I'm doing to help the Magi think.

(The children in the audience tap their chins and feet)

ADVENTURER 2
And finally…
(Pointing to one MAGI)
…one had a good gift and said, "Gold!"

(First MAGI says, "Gold!")

ADVENTURER 1
Another Magi…
(Pointing to another MAGI)
…had a good gift of oil and said, "Frankincense!"

(Second MAGI says, "Frankincense!")

ADVENTURER 2
And the last Magi…
(Pointing to the last MAGI)
…had a good gift of perfume and said, "Myrrh!"

(Third MAGI says, "Myrrh!")

ADVENTURER 1
And they knelt at Jesus's feet and gave him their gifts.

(ADVENTURERS encourage the MAGI to kneel)

ADVENTURER 2
Wow, those are great gifts. But we don't really have anything to give Jesus.
(To children in the audience)
Do you guys think Jesus would like video games?

(Children may respond)

ADVENTURER 1
Nah.

ADVENTURER 2
What about a puppy?

ADVENTURER 1
I don't think Jesus wants a puppy. Jesus is not a baby anymore.

ADVENTURER 2
I got it! A cell phone, or a laptop, or a car!

ADVENTURER 1
No, we don't have money to buy those things! Where can we find more about Jesus? Let's see what's in the bag.
(Pulls items out of bag)
A rock, a shoe…I was wondering where I put that, and the Bible.

ADVENTURER 2
(To children in the audience)
Which one do you think will tell me more about Jesus, the rock, the shoe, or the Bible?

(Children should scream, "Bible!")

ADVENTURER 1
The Bible is a great book to read if you want to know more about Jesus.
(To children in the audience)

Who wants to read with me in a loud voice John 3:16 to see what the Bible says about Jesus?

(Chooses a child from the audience to read)

For God so loved the world that he gave his one and only Son, that whosoever believes in him shall not perish but have eternal life.[7]

ADVENTURER 2

God gave his son Jesus as a gift to us?

ADVENTURER 1

Yes!

ADVENTURER 2

Great! I was worried because I have nothing to give Jesus. That was easy.

ADVENTURER 1

Wait! I remember reading something else in the Bible. (Shuffling through the Bible)

Here it is. Jesus said this when he was a grown up. Can someone help me read Mark 10:14 in a very loud voice?

(Chooses a child from the audience to read)

Let us read together, "Let the little children come to me and do not hinder them, for the kingdom of God belongs to such as these."[8]

---

[7] New International Version
[8] New International Version

ADVENTURER 2
Jesus wants children to come to him?

ADVENTURER 1
Yeah. You. Me. Every child. And all the people in here.

ADVENTURER 2
My gift is me!

ADVENTURER 1
Exactly! And my gift is me.
(To audience)
And your gift is you.

ADVENTURER 2
We learned so much today.

ADVENTURER 1
(To children in the audience)
We learned how Jesus, the Savior of the world, was born. We learned Jesus wants children to come to him. And we learned the Bible answers a lot of questions.

ADVENTURER 2
(To children in the audience)
Thank you so much for joining us! Give yourselves a round of applause.

ADVENTURER 1

(To children in the audience)

We hope to see you on our next adventure.

BOTH ADVENTURERS

(To children in the audience) Byeeeeee!

(Exit ADVENTURERS)

A Note from the Playwright

I am honored you have chosen *The Christmas Adventure* for your upcoming Christmas production!

This nativity drama is entertaining for children, parents, and actors. It's a fantastic way to teach young children about Jesus's birth and remind them of the importance of having Jesus in their lives.

To ensure that I can continue creating lively, biblically-based Christian plays for you and the children you serve, it is essential you purchase the performance license. The license legally authorizes you to produce the play. It also supports and encourages me as a playwright while helping me keep track of where *The Christmas Adventure* is being performed. The play has already been produced in the United States and the Caribbean. It makes me giddy thinking about all the places it can go!

To purchase your license for *The Christmas Adventure,* visit **www.JessicaBodiford.com**.

Have a blessed production and break a leg!

Jessica Bodiford

Made in United States
Orlando, FL
20 July 2022

19976264R00020